enjoy Playing the Cello

Margaret Martindale and Robert Cracknell

Note to the Teacher:

The cello is found today in many homes which have not had one before and in many schools which do not have a tradition of string-playing. *ENJOY PLAYING THE CELLO* is a resource of well-known tunes which are arranged so that music notation and a thorough knowledge of unextended first position are gradually introduced.

Fingerings and bowings are given for guidance but are not exclusive. To aid intonation the early pieces have accompaniments for a second cello to be played by the teacher or a more advanced student. In later pieces, the more adventurous may like to improvise simple accompaniments. Some of the tunes have been slightly simplified.

M.M.
R.C.

Music Department
OXFORD UNIVERSITY PRESS
Oxford and New York

CONTENTS

Oxford University Press, Great Clarendon Street, Oxford OX2 6DP
Oxford University Press Inc., 198 Madison Avenue, New York, NY 10016, USA

Oxford is a trade mark of Oxford University Press

© *Oxford University Press 1989*

1 FIRST NOTES

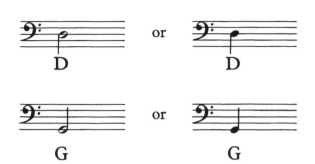

or

D   D

or

G   G

PATTERNS

1

2

3

4

Nut Tree

Traditional

Bass

Tune

(V)

Any old iron

Charles Collins, F. A. Sheppard,
Fred Terry

Roll out the barrel

Lew Brown, Wladimir A. Timm,
Jaromir Vejuoda

2 FIRST FINGERS

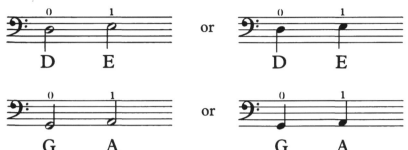 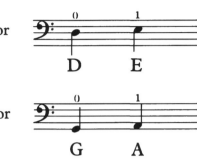

PATTERNS

1

2

3

4

This old man

Traditional

Michael Finnegan

Traditional

Bass

Tune

There is a tavern in the town

Cornish Folksong

Bass

Tune

Yankee Doodle

Traditional

Bass

Tune

3 THE A STRING

PATTERNS

William Tell

Gioacchino Rossini
(1792–1868)

A Tune by Schubert

Franz Schubert
(1797–1828)

Waltzing Matilda

Marie Cowan

On Ilkley Moor

Traditional

8

4 SHARPS

D E F♯
(F sharp)

A B C♯
(C sharp)

PATTERNS

1

2

3

4

Hunting song

Traditional

Merrily we roll along

Traditional

Merrily – Again

Traditional

Old MacDonald

Traditional

5 FOURTH FINGERS

G

D

PATTERNS

◻ = DOWN BOW (Pull)   ∨ = UP BOW (Push)

1

2

3

4

TUNES FROM DIFFERENT COUNTRIES

Holland – Carol

Traditional

France – au clair de la lune

Traditional

* Originally:

Hungary — Folk song

Traditional

Russia — Folk dance

Traditional

America — Aunt Rhody

Traditional

6 LOW NOTES AND QUICK NOTES

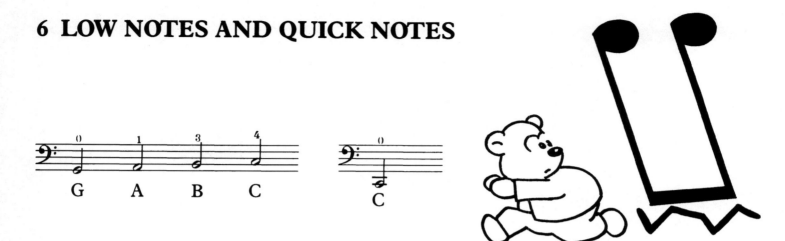

G   A   B   C

C

PATTERNS

1

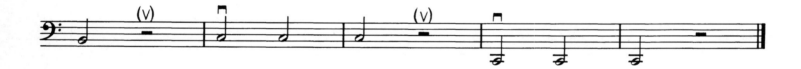

2

3

The Drunken Sailor

Sea shanty

Tom Dooley

Traditional American

Camptown Races

Stephen Foster (1826–64)

Lulu

Billy Rose, Lew Brown,
Ray Henderson

7 THREE IN A BAR

PATTERNS

Blow the man down

Sea shanty

London's burning

Traditional

Oh, dear! What can the matter be?

Old English song

Morning has broken

Traditional

Ludwig

Drink to me only with thine eyes

Traditional

8 DOTS, AND SOME MORE LOW NOTES

PATTERNS

Michael, row the boat ashore

Spiritual

Kookaburra's Song

Traditional

Greensleeves

Traditional

Puff, the magic dragon

Peter Yarrow

* Originally: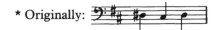

18

Can-Can

Jacques Offenbach (1819–80)

Frère Jacques

Traditional

Augustin

Traditional

Cockles and mussels

Traditional Irish

9 SECOND FINGERS

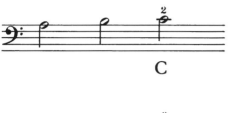

C

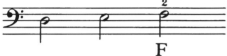

F

PATTERNS

Supercalifragilisticexpialidocious

Richard M. Sherman,
Robert B. Sherman

John Peel

Traditional

Villikins

Traditional

Red River Valley

Traditional American

Lilliburlero

Traditional

My old man's a dustman

Lonnie Donegan

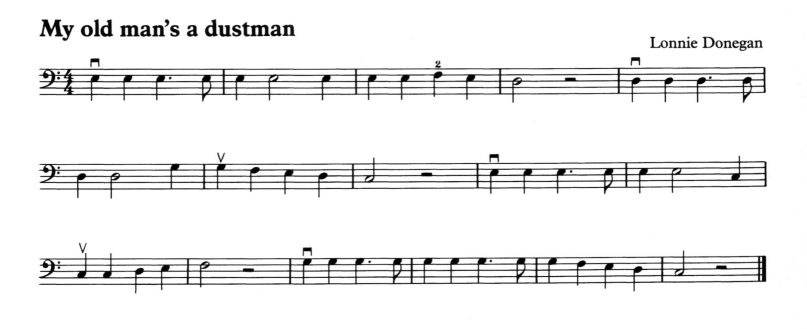

St. Anthony Chorale

Traditional

TUNES TO PLAY, USING 2nd AND 3rd FINGERS

Early one morning

Traditional

Sucking Cider

Based on 'The Lone Fish Ball'

Daisy, Daisy

Traditional

The Ash Grove

Traditional

Polly-Wolly-Doodle

Traditional

The Yellow Rose of Texas

Traditional

Skip to my Lou

Traditional

10 TWO IN A BAR

PATTERNS

Nuts in May

Traditional

The Farmer's in his den

Traditional

Yankee Doodle

Traditional

Oats, Peas, Beans

Traditional

Short'nin' Bread

American work song

Dargason

Traditional

Farandole

Georges Bizet (1838–75)

Nelly the elephant

Ralph Butler, Peter Hart

German folk-song

Traditional

The Teddy Bears' Picnic

John W. Bratton
James B. Kennedy

11 SLURS

PATTERNS

Alouette

Traditional

My Grandfather's clock

Henry C. Work

Country Gardens

Traditional

The Vicar of Bray

17th century

The Quartermaster's Stores

Traditional

Flow gently, sweet Afton

Traditional

12 MORE SLURS, AND A NEW NOTE

G   A   B♭
(B flat)

PATTERNS

London Bridge

Traditional

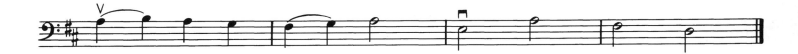

Polly, put the kettle on

Traditional

Golden Slumbers

Traditional

Cradle Song

Johannes Brahms (1833–97)

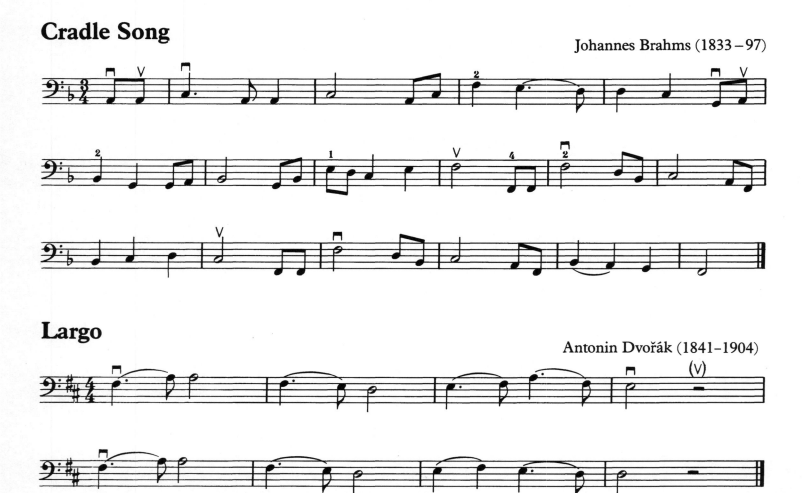

Largo

Antonin Dvořák (1841–1904)

Looby Loo

Traditional

Rule Britannia

Thomas Arne (1710–78)

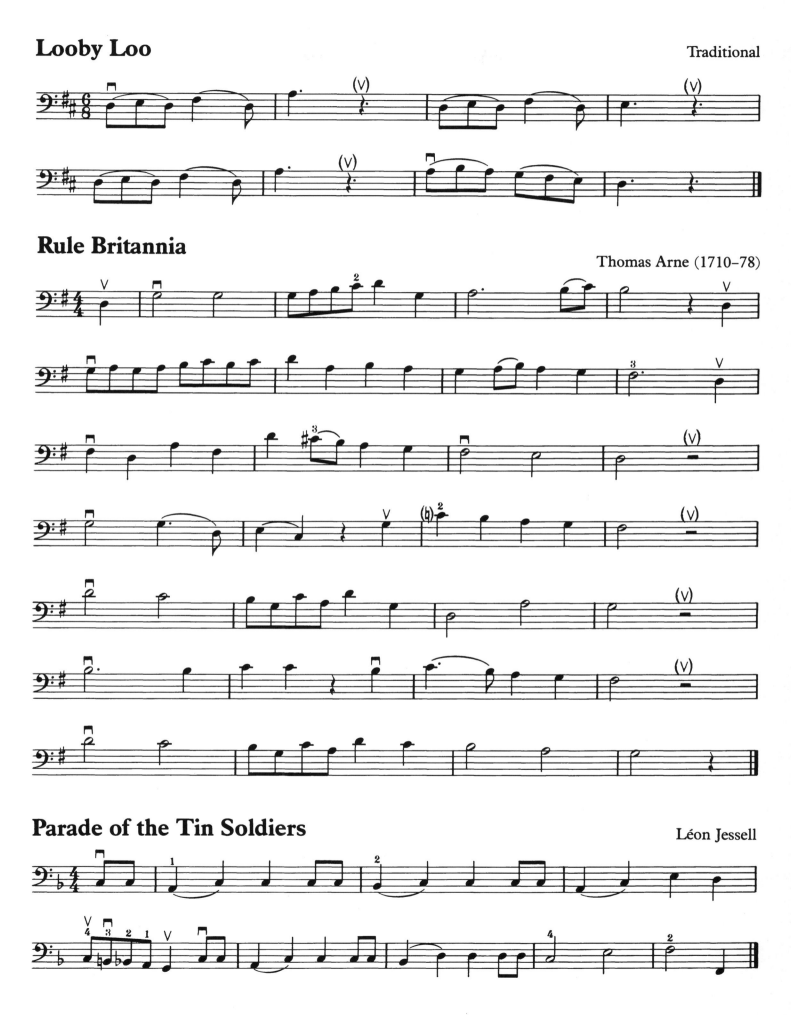

Parade of the Tin Soldiers

Léon Jessell

MORE TUNES TO PLAY

Hornpipe

Traditional

Rakes of Mallow

Traditional

Jimmy crack corn

Traditional

The British Grenadiers

Traditional

Pack up your troubles

Felix Powell

Tune from 'The Nutcracker'

Peter Tchaikovsky (1840–93)

Barbara Allen

Traditional

Oh! Susanna

Traditional

The Elephant

Camille Saint-Saëns (1835–1921)

13 MORE DOTS

PATTERNS

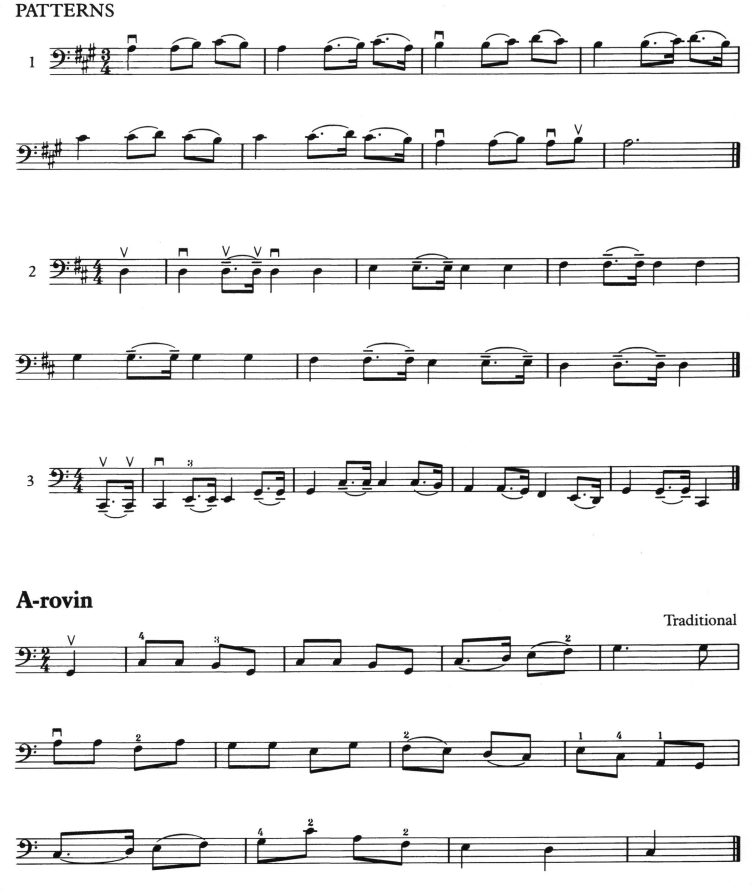

A-rovin

Traditional

Kum-ba-ya

Spiritual

Show me the way to go home

Irving King

Notice that 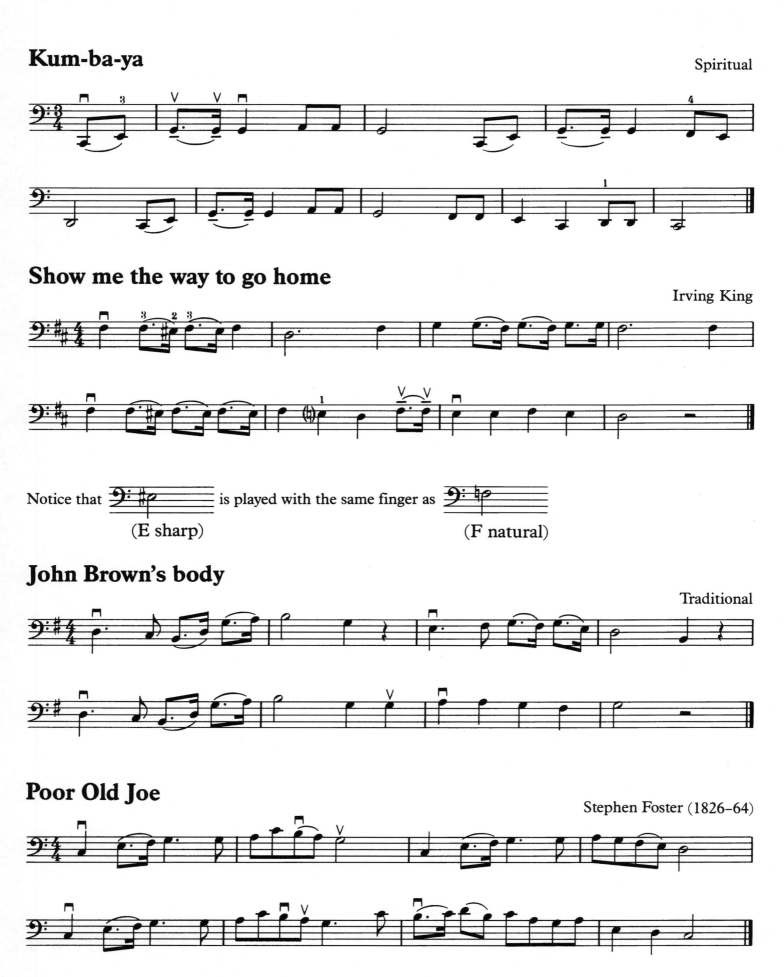 (E sharp) is played with the same finger as (F natural)

John Brown's body

Traditional

Poor Old Joe

Stephen Foster (1826–64)

Loch Lomond

Traditional Scottish

Clementine

Traditional

A Tune by Mozart

Wolfgang Mozart (1756–91)

She'll be coming round the mountain

Traditional

14 OFF THE BEAT

PATTERNS

Round and round the village

Traditional

Nobody knows

Traditional

Mocking Bird

Traditional

Swanee River

Stephen Foster (1826–64)

Swing low, sweet chariot

Spiritual

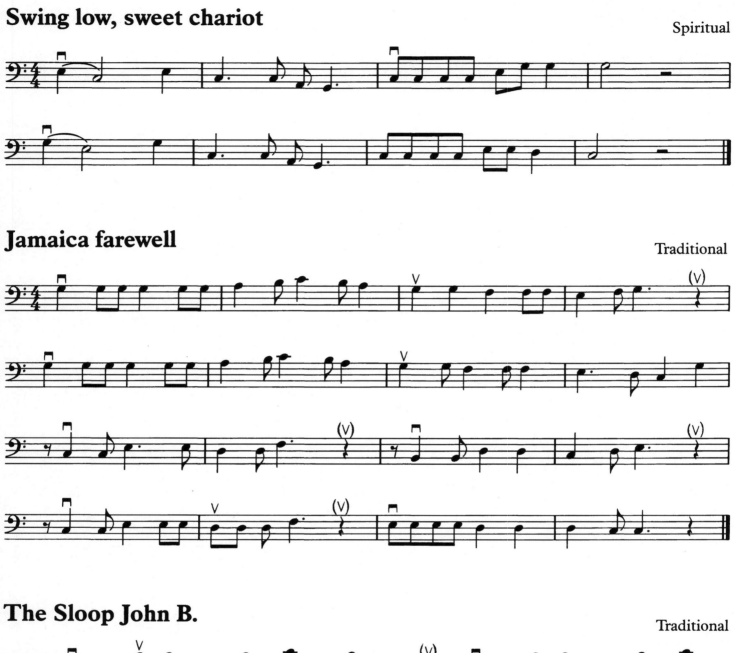

Jamaica farewell

Traditional

The Sloop John B.

Traditional

DANCE DUETS

Waltz – Roses from the South

Johann Strauss II (1825–99)

Ragtime

Mátyás Seiber (1905–60)

Tune

Bass

pizz.

Gavotte

Johann Sebastian Bach
(1685–1750)

Tune

Bass

Clarinet Quintet Minuet

Wolfgang Mozart (1756–91)

44

Samba – Mango Walk

Traditional

Tune

Bass

pizz.

arco

+

Song of the King (Rock)

Music: Andrew Lloyd Webber
Lyrics: Tim Rice

Tune

Bass

Printed in England by Caligraving Limited Thetford Norfolk

INDEX